12 DAYS OF

Sexmas

A CHRISTMAS GIFT FOR

FROM

12 DAYS OF

Sexmas

DAY

This coupon is good for...

A Long, Passionate Kiss

I WANT TO FEEL YOU AS CLOSE TO ME AS POSSIBLE. LET'S KISS!!

12 DAYS OF

Sexmas

DAY

This coupon is good for...

Have a Movie Night

LET'S COPY SOME OF THE MOVES FROM YOUR FAVORITE PORNO.

12 DAYS OF

Sexmas

DAY

3

This coupon is good for...

Morning Time Oral Pleasure

I WILL WAKE YOU UP WITH MY MOUTH , TONGUE AND LIPS.

12 DAYS OF

Sexmas

DAY

4

This coupon is good for...

A Slippery, Oily Massage

I CAN'T THINK OF ANYTHING SEXIER THAN SEEING
YOU NAKED AND SHINY WITH BODY OIL.

12 DAYS OF

DAY

This coupon is good for...

All Clean, Now Get Dirty

TAKE ME INTO THE BATHTUB OR SHOWER AND
LET ME WASH YOU FROM HEAD TO TOE.

12 DAYS OF

Sexmas

DAY

This coupon is good for...

Be a Dom / Sub

LET ME SUBMIT TO YOU FOR A NIGHT. I WANT TO PLEASE YOU!

12 DAYS OF

Sexmas

DAY

This coupon is good for...

Sexy Lingerie

LET ME WEAR SOMETHING NEW AND SEXY FOR YOU. YOUR CHOICE!

12 DAYS OF

 *Sexmas*

DAY

This coupon is good for...

New Positions, Better Opportunity

IS THERE A WAY THAT YOU WANT TO SEE ME THAT'S BEEN ON YOUR MIND?
LET'S LOOK INTO SOME NEW POSITIONS!

12 DAYS OF

Sexmas

DAY

 9

This coupon is good for...

An Erotic Strip Tease

YOU HAVE MY FULL ATTENTION TONIGHT,
AND I'M GOING TO SHOW YOU BY GIVING YOU A SEXY STRIPTEASE.

12 DAYS OF

DAY

10

This coupon is good for...

Food Served on Your Body

I WANT TO LICK YOU UP AND DOWN WHILE YOU'RE COVERED IN SWEETS!

12 DAYS OF

 *Sexmas*

DAY

(11)

This coupon is good for...

All Tied Up

A NIGHT OF BEING AT YOUR MERCY SOUNDS EQUALLY FUN AND SEXY!

12 DAYS OF

Sexmas

DAY

This coupon is good for...

A Fantasy Role Play

LET'S ACT OUT A DEEP, DARK FANTASY OF YOURS!

12 DAYS OF

 Sexmas

Made in the USA
Las Vegas, NV
02 December 2024

13155924R00024